WE LEFT THE
CAMP SINGING

WE LEFT THE CAMP SINGING

The Etty Hillesum Poems and Drawings

JANICE KULYK KEEFER

CLAIRE WILKS

PREFACE BY

DIANA KUPREL

EXILE editions

Publishers of Singular

Fiction, Poetry, Nonfiction, Translation, Drama and Graphic Books

Library and Archives Canada Cataloguing in Publication

Keefer, Janice Kulyk, 1952-, author
We left the camp singing : the Etty Hillesum poems and drawings /
Janice Kulyk Keefer ; Claire Wilks, artist ; preface by Diana Kuprel.

Issued in print and electronic formats.
ISBN 978-1-55096-802-6 (softcover).--ISBN 978-1-55096-803-3 (EPUB).--
ISBN 978-1-55096-804-0 (Kindle).--ISBN 978-1-55096-805-7 (PDF)

1. Hillesum, Etty, 1914-1943--Poetry. 2. Holocaust, Jewish
(1939-1945)--Netherlands--Poetry. 3. Holocaust, Jewish (1939-1945), in
art. 4. Drawing, Canadian--21st century. I. Kuprel, Diana, 1963-, writer
of preface II. Wilks, Claire, 1933-2017, artist III. Title.

PS8571.E435W45 2018   C811'.54   C2018-904710-0
                                            C2018-904711-9

Published by Exile Editions Ltd ~ www.ExileEditions.com
144483 Southgate Road 14 – GD, Holstein, Ontario, N0G 2A0
Printed and Bound in Canada by Marquis.

We gratefully acknowledge the Canada Council for the Arts,
the Government of Canada, the Ontario Arts Council,
and the Ontario Media Development Corporation
for their support toward our publishing activities.

Canadian sales representation:
The Canadian Manda Group, 664 Annette Street,
Toronto ON M6S 2C8 www.mandagroup.com 416 516 0911

North American and international distribution, and U.S. sales:
Independent Publishers Group, 814 North Franklin Street,
Chicago IL 60610 www.ipgbook.com toll free: 1 800 888 4741

for

Britta Olinder and Conny Steenman-Marcusse

Contents

PREFACE
by Diana Kuprel

On October 7, 1943, a young Dutch woman named Esther "Etty" Hillesum (1914-1943) tossed a postcard from the train that was transporting her and her family from the transit camp of Westerbork to the concentration camp of Auschwitz. Found by Dutch farmers, who diligently posted it, it read: *"Opening the Bible at random I find this: 'The Lord is my high tower'. I am sitting on my rucksack in the middle of a full freight car. Father, Mother, and Mischa [her younger brother] are a few cars away. In the end, the departure came without warning... We left the camp singing... Thank you for all your kindness and care."* None of her family – neither her parents nor her two brothers, the elder of whom was later transported to Bergen Belsen – would survive the Holocaust. Etty perished in Auschwitz on November 30, 1943.

The postcard gives this collection of poems by Janice Kulyk Keefer, and of drawings and monoprints by Claire Wilks, its title. The diaries and confessional letters that Etty wrote during World War II – and that record both the oppression of Jewish people in Amsterdam during the German occupation, as well as Etty's religious awakening – give it its springboard. "We left the camp singing..." is an astonishing response, in word and image, to Etty's exterior and interior life and an utterly singular work of art in the canon of the Shoah. It is a fierce avowal of creativity and selfhood against one of the most ferociously dehumanizing acts in the history of humanity. It is an astounding performance of ontological vehemence that rescues life from annihilation. It is attestation in the face of the ultimate test.

The poetry is in three parts – the first two in Etty's voice, the last in the poet's.

"Amsterdam," the longest part, is unflinching in its depiction of the increasingly brutal and systematic persecution of the Jewish population. It opens with a gesture of defiance as it moves from the universal – there have been wars through the ages, "as many wars as there are worlds" – to the particular of this war, this place, this woman. The exterior conditions counterpoint a subtle interplay of eros and ethics in the portrayal of Etty's discovery and claiming of her sexuality, sensuality and sense of self as an intellectual and writer, her deepening faith in God as a power to be nurtured in oneself, and her commitment to reaching out beyond herself. It is a portrayal of a self that cannot be thought without alterity – whether that other is the experience of one's own body as flesh, the experience of love in intersubjective relationships, or the experience of conscience and of God.

The second part, "Westerbork," conveys – in seven devastatingly blunt poems – her internment in the transit camp where she had once worked, believing it was her duty "to be of some use to others," and her acceptance of, and preparation for, the inevitability of extinction.

In "Poland," the briefest, Kulyk Keefer pivots the perspective and turns to Etty, questioning her whether she was able, in the end, to keep faith with her hard-won conception, and love, of God, without which she would experience a double annihilation.

The poems, so excruciating in their bearing of witness, are accompanied by Wilks' equally haunting, deeply humane and unabashedly sensual conté crayon drawings and monoprints.

In her Etty series, with line only – and what a masterful, unerring and evocative stroke she possesses – Wilks bursts the boundaries of the sheet, even as she restrains, constrains, intertwines and enframes the straining bodies. With great tenderness and empathy, Wilks renders, in her distinctive visual language, resistance against oppression and annihilation through the exuberant claiming of sexuality. As she wrests being from nothingness, she turns the regard of the figures so fully inwardly as to be self-suffused, in defiant disregard of the gaze of others.

Where the drawings give figuration to Etty's self, to what Aleksandr Ti ma (the author of *The Use of Man* and *Kapo*, novels about the Second World War) has so insightfully called "the singing in the flesh," the monoprints render an instant of ambiguity, the uneasy equilibrium between being and non-being, between acting and being acted upon that is the essence of suffering. One is never certain whether the figure is emerging, as if being birthed, or is being scratched and abraded, its contours deprived of what might distinguish it, grasped ominously by hands that could appear to be "the claw of a bird of prey" drawing the figure back into oblivion.

Still, as these works express, even in places of immense suffering – like the Tod-fabrik, which in Kulyk Keefer's words "is also life" – where the self is forbidden to occupy the place of foundation, there is simultaneously a supreme faith in the embodied self, the self as flesh and fount of creativity.

Kulyk Keefer and Wilks do dare to throw down the gauntlet to the forces of mass annihilation.

In her final gesture, the poet gives Etty the last word, enjoining the reader as she links the act and challenge of bearing witness to the expression of this hope, this profound conviction in creativity:

"If one only becomes creative,
even in one's saddest and most desperate moments,
then surely nothing else matters?
And a creative moment is surely not paid for
too dearly with suffering?"

The Croatian poet Slavko Mihailić once wrote of Wilks, in his piece "Rediscovery of the Human Body": "Her art is singular, requiring no outside authority." I would dare to claim the same of this singular collaboration of word and image, which has been birthed seemingly inexplicably in this strange hinterland that is Toronto – a city far from the arena in which the Holocaust was played out, and yet to which these two remarkable artists, likewise born in this hinterland, are inextricably enjoined by blood, by roots, indeed by conscience.

Etty Hillesum
1914–1943

Let the stars of its dawn be dark;
let it hope for light, but have none, nor see the eyelids of the morning.

Job 3:9

Hineinhorchen

Italicized passages used in the poems are quotations and close readings
drawn from *Etty: The Letters and Diaries of Etty Hillesum 1941-1943*.

ONE

Amsterdam

*I would be happy washing dishes
for a living, as long as I had a field
of study of my own.*

Circumstances

War, the Second World.
As if there haven't been hundreds
before: ask the Carthaginians,
the Aztecs, ask the Neanderthals
—as many wars as there are worlds.

Amsterdam, during the Second World War.
Occupation: resistance.
Executions: screams across the heath;
strangled interrogations.

A Jew, in Amsterdam, during the Second World War.
Roaring trade in yellow cloth, earthbound
constellations. Rationing, registrations,
round-ups.

A Jewish woman in Amsterdam during the Second World War.
Age, 27. Unmarried, childless, no occupation
in particular. A law degree, a love
of Rilke and Russian; a view
out a window at Gabrielmetsustraat, 6
(the Rijksmuseum flanked by trees).
Heart unencumbered, soul
one block of black granite.

Portrait of the Writer as an Old Soul

A Turkish rug for a curtain.
On the wall, a fierce Moroccan girl—a photo,
torn from a magazine. On my desk
a typewriter, cigarettes, this exercise book,
this little coat hanger *from which*
a whole evening—a single hour—
hangs

No lady at window:
no letter, no spinet,

no pearls.

Sinnbild

Each waking
a birth from night's warm belly.

Chill of a damp, grey day:
a bright shawl over my terra cotta-coloured sweater.

Queues for butter, queues for bread.
That bolt of gypsy cloth I saved.

Yellow stars, regulation height, width, stitch.
A dress *open on all sides to the sun, the wind and his caresses.*

Forbidden trains, trams, bicycles.
A whole summer on the heath,

me in the gypsy dress with tanned,
bare legs and flowing gypsy hair

and then a small farmhouse with a low-beamed ceiling
and the smell of apples, and a view over the heath at night.

Through ocean's grey eternity,
my narrow boat.

Birth of an Uncarried Child

Ten days since I first knew
you were alive.

At fourteen I went to watch
my mother at the asylum. You could
not call it visiting. My brothers
checked themselves in and out of the ward
as if it were a hotel:
big spenders.

Käthe, who weeps
over what's become of her *Heimat,*
warms the towels, scalds water, secures
quinine. You gush

into this madness
innocent of flag or star
or life.

Wrestling Match with Julius

Integral Part of the Treatment:
analyst, analysand getting down to basics
(viz. the floor: bare, unswept).

Playfully, at first, and then to win.
Massive man, mere woman
(half his age, his bulk)

I floored him, then
dabbed his split lip with cologne. I,

orderer of chaos, reclaimer of land
from raging seas, dauntless
darner of stockings,

more than a match for a balding, half-deaf
refugee: more wisdom
in one of his eyebrow hairs
than in whole libraries.

Unleashing, in that clumsy dust and sweat
that final, liberating scream
that always sticks bashfully in your throat
when you make love.

Daily Round

Wake, wash, write.

Prepare breakfast for the household
with Käthe's help

(Käthe, our German cook,
teaches me how to make mock
whipped cream.)

Return to my room to study Old Slavonic.
Lunch.
Teach Russian to my merchant from
Enkhuizen, who brings us sacks of gold
disguised as beans. Teach Russian
to that bold young woman
with the sleek head of a boy.

Cross 5 streets, 1 bridge
and 2 canals to Courbetstraat.
Transcribe his shorthand notes:
all the cries and cramps
of the souls he cares for.

A little wrestling, a little nestling,
then home to peel vegetables for supper.
Reading by the stove, or out
to our only concert halls:
our friends' cramped parlours.

Home, bath, book—perhaps
the telephone, his voice through the wire
close enough to stroke my throat.

To bed with Han, or better,
the narrowness of my solitary cot. Shedding
the day with my clothes, diving clean
into dark.

Our Common Fate

Everyone who seeks to save himself
must surely realize that if he does not go,
another must take his place.
As if it mattered which of us goes.

To harass, to humiliate,
beat and break us. To plunder,
enslave, strip us bare. But

to annihilate? Each one of us,
senile and foetal,
parent and child.

I will not hide myself
like a rat in a wall. I refuse
a job's short safety,
selling my people in job lots.

Let others launch their leaky rafts.
I will join all those
on their backs, in this vast
sea, staring up at the sky

going down with prayer
on their lips

My naked feet
on iron ground

their lips.

Palm Reader

Julius, you ladies' man, you troll, you
bluff, big-bellied, *biscuit-loving uncle,*
50-year-old clod of earth.
Roman Emperor or mere Olympian?
Sultan whose passions swell the curve
of your lower lip, the right-hand corner.

God-seeker, God-giver, teacher
of the act and need of prayer.
Sitting with you at the dinner table,
your face washed with moonlight, young
as a crocus.

You have only to stretch out your arms
for women's breasts to home to your hands.
The heavy fullness of your mouth, suppleness
of tongue. Confiding
that you never masturbate after
saying your prayers; lecturing me
on the precise function of the clitoris.

I never worshipped you: you
invaded me. In spite of your pale and faraway,
your sad, saved fiancée, I was intent
we should marry, just
to face Poland, together.

Even that longing fell from me.
I no longer desired you, but knew you. Not
the false teeth, hearing aid,
the way you sing, *like an old lion who's
stepped on a razor blade,*

but the grey landscape
of your face, the tired lakes of your eyes,
older than I will ever be:

the greatest
and deepest happiness of my life
sipping your breath
from the beaker of your mouth.

Alchemy

To belong to one's experience. And to transform it.

Turning shit to gold. Jackboots
to bare & blistered feet.

To make the vulnerable
strong, to give the beaten
the ultimate
and only form of power:

to forgive.

Life

I am not I, there is nothing
to which I need put my name.

Nothing to do or say to show
I am worthy to have lived.

I need know nothing, understand
nothing.

At my feet, a feather:
Eternity.

With Liesl at the Dressmaker's

small bird,
    moonlight bather on warm
        summer nights

yet strong enough to clean
spinach 3 hours each day;
queue another 3 for bread.

Two young children, a husband
whose hand running down my face
is the claw of a bird of prey.

I draw you to me in my sleep,
wake in a shudder of flesh.

Lover I will never lie with,
my only girlfriend,
small Liesl
who will outlive us all.

A Vast and Fruitful Loneliness

I love to be alone so much. And...
we Jews are being crowded
into ever smaller spaces.

All the roads inside me, the endless
highways, the gates You unlocked—
How much space there was for me.

Plain, heath, so easily crossed:
soul's native land, the vast
horizons of one's whole life,
only just
opening.

Inside me a rapacious sea
and the fistful of land I've reclaimed.

Just before waking, I feel, inside me
spaces and distances locked up
wanting to break out, to unfold
into ever wider spaces and distances

feel them like the necks of horses
stamping and pawing in a crowded stable

infinite steppes spread out inside me:
their wind on my face, their earth.

Ascetic

I study
how to be hungry. How
to be cold, dirty, a prey to lice.
How to unlearn comfort. Comfort takes
too much energy; mourning its loss
takes too much time.

I practise nakedness,
disrobing myself of the day, entering night
the way one slips into a bath, needing
and having nothing.

Day's dirt and fears: something
to let drop, subject
to the gravity of these times.

I am learning to remember
hyacinth-scented soap, cashmere or
crèpe de chine against my skin.

Each new day, a garment
so rich, so unexpected
I cannot tell whether to tug it
over my head, or
inch inside.

Jasmine, from the Balcony

So radiant, so virginal.
An exuberant young bride lost
in a back street.

Do not grieve that you cannot take in
the beauty of jasmine. No need.
Miracles cancel the need for belief.

Soon lice will be eating us up in Poland;
storms will bruise the jasmine—drowned shreds
in mud-pools on the garage roof—

while somewhere inside me
jasmine will bloom undisturbed,
profuse, delicate. That jasmine:

it has been there
a long time—but only now
are words beginning to fail me
about it.

Room

Beloved stove, grey day,
whimpering stomach, woollen dress,
slim, strong hand.

My everywhere: my desert island,
convent cell with a view
onto anything I wish to see:
cornfields or a caliph's palace.

Crammed bookcase: one huge, layered mind.
Desk: my true half, my trusty bicycle's
second self.

I carry you inside me on streets I walk
till my heels run blood. I will keep you
in barracks crammed
with plank beds, matchstick bodies.

Each morning, one
silent hour here: six minutes
or sixty. Foundation of all that follows:

If I don't work every moment,
make use of this time with all
my energy and concentration

I will have lived even less
than what's been granted me.

Between Sleep and Waking

a moment when all heaviness falls away,
when life is so indescribably
good and light to bear that it seems
sheer surface—a glittering, bright
wide plain.

Sheer surface exists no more than peace.
I know this: there are
caves and caverns, too,
though to describe them so
turns them into something out of
fairy tales, or Mendelssohn.

Caves are cold, deep, dank,
dark. You cannot see to read;
you cannot move to write.

The night they issued the decree
(for our heads heaped on platters)
we sat on comfortable chairs
(bought with insurance money against bomb damage).

Philosophising together, drinking real coffee,
we could not have been happier.
Cave dwellers. Skaters.

Sun Lounge

In a northern country known
for brisk winds, this
ripe pleasure:
sun full on my face, my bare feet,
as I talk with friends, breaking
the bread of the day.

Confirmed voluptuary,
seasoned lover,
bosom-shaking dancer,

abandoned ascetic.
Fiery marrow, fleshy
bones.

In the Ice Cream Parlour

Wall-to-wall yellow. Sunlight trapped
in cream. We sit and eat,

having just signed
(polite, with smiles)
our death warrants, in the Gestapo Hall.

This place is cosy as the cloth
from which we cut our stars, the warm coats
to which we stitch them.

Useless,
imagining the kind of dark
they'll light, one day.
Why turn sugar-cream
to wax and ashes?

Sufficient unto each day
the evil thereof.

Vanilla, chocolate, licorice.

Rumours and Reports

One must not die while still alive,
One has to live one's life to the full
And to the end.

Mind stumbles to the door they're beating;
listens carefully, keeps them
off the threshold. Body

betrays, lets them in to shit on the rug,
torch the beams or hack them
into a thousand splinters: *each piece*
has a different pain.

If they are true, we can do nothing.
If false, they're strong enough
to poison sleep.

There will always be suffering—
What difference whether from this or that?

Leave us at least the little hope
we have left, the little time.

But when they call up
girls of sixteen, when the whole
earth becomes one prison camp.
When the Germans—so the story goes—
bury us alive or kill us with gas

leave us, at least, some small grace
in suffering.

Time

In two years,
from minute to minute,
you can live a long life.

Reading Rilke, St. Augustine.
Queuing, by starlight, for the belief

that even in the last moment
of the most terrible death,
life has been good.

From heartbeat to heartbeat:
immersion in this now, this here. Still,

there's Russia, there's heaven:
distant horizons that lie
beyond these days.

Telephone

Each time you call, Beloved—
an adventure.

Who knew how Bacchic
that stern, black instrument could be?

Wires so sensitive they fingerprint
the thrum of a throat.

A different voice, a different ring
in the daytime, than in the evening:

before I pick it up, I always know
whether it's life, or death.

Too Much Reality

A poem by Rilke is real and as important
as a young man falling out of an airplane.
All that happens, happens in this world of ours
and you must not leave one thing out
for the sake of another.

So let us be jugglers, God.
Ambidextrous
Siamese twins, alchemists
turning earth to air, blood
to something clearer than water;

granite
to flesh, and flesh to prayer,

a cheese coupon
into one line from *The Book of Hours*.

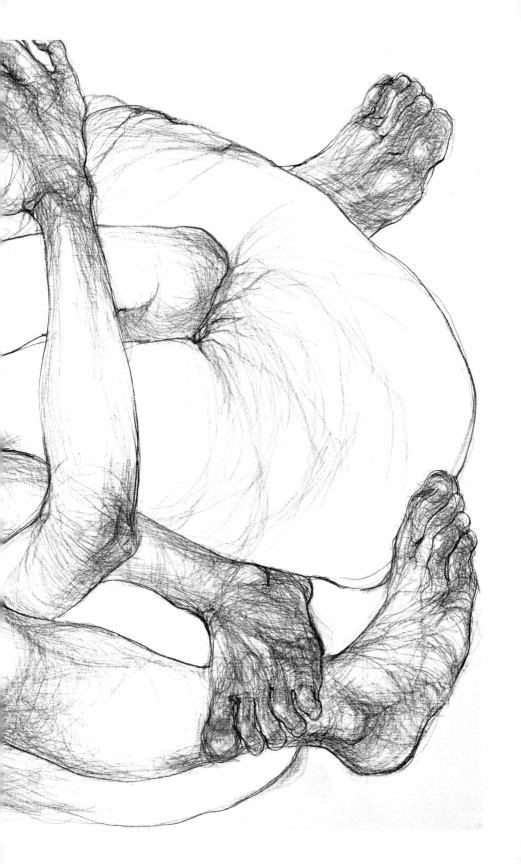

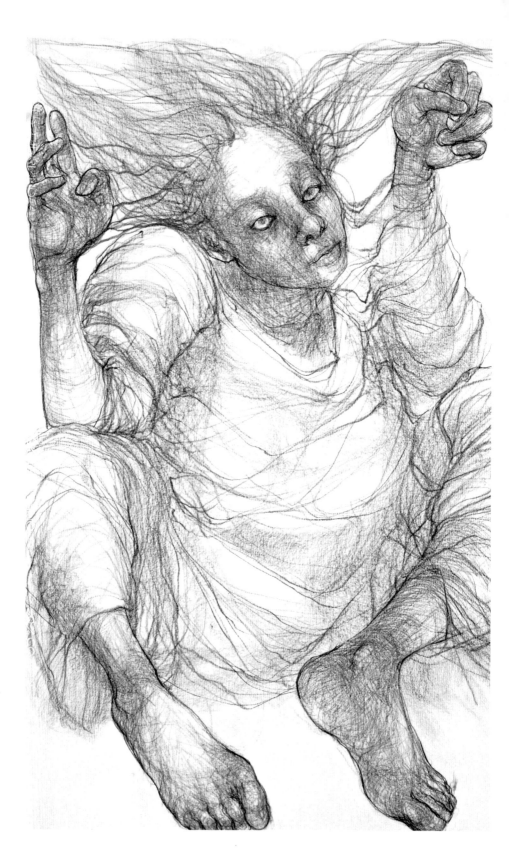

Hineinhorchen

That German for which, again,
there's no Dutch word.

Laying your ear
against your own breast,

not thinking:
inlistening—

sensing the slow, dark ripening:
soul's free and full surrender.

The pause between two breaths
hearkens unto itself, and unto others,

unto God, the spirit
in me, God
to God.

Stadionkade

My wrung-out belly,
bandaged
by a hot water bottle. Chilblains
gouging my feet;
a woollen shawl on my clotted head.

All the better to see you with, my dear,
dear steppes of the Skating Club grounds:
stripped, snow-blind.

On your sands we walked and walked,
discussing poetry, he with a tin of condensed milk
bought in a perfume shop, I
with a bag of golden rennet apples.

Such swag! Such boundlessness!
Carrying milk and apples,
knowing, suddenly,
that beyond this, there is
nothing more. What is,

the vastness of what is. Then,
nothing.

The Patient

(From *patior*: Latin, deponent verb.
Meaning: 'I suffer' or 'it is suffered by me.')

<u>Ills of the Body</u>
Leaden fatigue.
Headache, restlessness,
severe menstrual pains.
Erotic greed.

<u>Ills of the Mind</u>
Stone-sadness, anxiety, fear:
(madness in the family: schizophrenia,
to be doctrinaire).

<u>Ills of the Heart</u>
A coward, a dullard who has yet
to make a friend of any stranger, to give
an Other root-room in a heart
that's no mere
flower pot.

<u>Ills of the Soul</u>
Spiritual constipation, civil
war between head and heart. Waste,
chaos: self a mere bag of
spikes, shards.
Shame.

<u>Cure</u>
Unclench, one by one
soul's small, stiff fingers. Dig
the way diviners do. Through dirt to liquid
crystal.

. . .

Uncover your gift, what
you will do with your life.
Help others, clouded, shattered
as you are, to that honesty called clarity.

Speak and write words
of fired ice, their truth close
as leaves pressed against
a window.

Become complete, whole, a
human being. No fear
of really being nothing but
a ridiculous amateur.

Self & Others

If I don't start with myself,
how can I change anything for the better?
If I don't know myself,
how can I understand others

just as confused and weak, just
as helpless as me? Even that young
Gestapo officer shouting at me
had more need of my compassion
than I of his.

It is not in my nature *to hate*
any human being for his so-called wickedness.
Injustice, suffering
move me to pity, not rage (though
I denounce with the best and worst).

A little peace, a lot of kindness,
and a little wisdom.

Prayer

I.

Sitting on the dustbin
on the small, stony terrace.
Hidden, head leaning
against the washtub, sun stoking
my black hair, my white eyelids.

The map my mind draws, from the bare
branches of the chestnut, to the rasp
of sparrows. Tracing all angles and objects,
reading each furrow of tree bark, until something

(more and less
than that push
from my mother's salt sea)

occurs in me, occurs,
deep down. As a child
taking up her first crayon, draws
not this or that
but colour itself, in
and as
itself.

II.

Eyes cast down, not heavenwards.
Pretending, when someone walks by,
to look for a button burst from a coat.

The girl who learned to pray,
forced to her knees by something
stronger, better than herself:

by the doors blown off
the chaos within.

III.

Uncork this bottle,
shame-stoppered.
Embed this gesture
into bone and flesh.

My bone,
my flesh.

Between bed and bookcase,
room enough to bend, knees clasping floor,
fingers interlaced: strong shoots:
willow or the rushes splayed
across the bottom of the broken chair.

My body's laws of gravity and need:
lead weights, to make drapes hang true.
Jewels sewn in the seams of a refugee's coat.

Holding the book of my face, my hands.
Closer than any nakedness
before a new lover:

prayer threading the maze to my self
and You.

At the Pharmacy

Where, trying to buy toothpaste,
I am grilled by *someone in the shape
of a fellow human being.*

"Are you permitted to—?" the word, *Jew,*
implied.
"Yes, sir. This is a pharmacy." I answer
softly, firmly, in my customary
pleasant manner.

He stomps off, cheated of the chance
to show his civic zeal. If only
I'd been fingering melons
at the greengrocers, he
could have hauled me off,
polished his pride
on my soft,
yet firm,
yellow star.

Night

Trapped in a cage. Iron walls,
my arms, beating—

Always, at night, an open window
ever a new night, over and over again.

Every landscape on this planet
in the always-different sky.

One has what wings one needs to fly across any walls
into a sky that knows of no...partitions.

Orchard Light

Stars catch in the bare trees
outside my window; glisten
like pears or apples picked
in some hungerless paradise.

They catch, then climb free,
or graze heaven's plain.

In a strange house, in a strange bed,
I take down the blackout paper, hear
two stars speaking:

"Wherever you are in the world
you will find us, always; know
yourself home."

Music

We give the cold shoulder
to the Concertgebouw; prefer
our Schubert sung with a slap of Yiddish.

My brother plays with intensity, they say,
and his usual cool brilliance. Only I can see
how his hands pray to the piano.

And now my palm reader, with the dear,
dubious voice, goes on forever.
Patience!
Think of how, the last soirée

that lady of high nobility with the rich
profusion of blond curls on her forehead
sang like a Japanese
canary in labour.

Mystic

Cycling home from Courbetstraat, last night:
my arms, my hair, my thighs
streaming tenderness, everything
I could not give him.

At the little bridge over the canal,
I stood looking at the water, spring's
arms around me as I poured
all this love I could not show or speak
into starry water.

What is, what must be:
to vanish into the vastness of air, to break
the I through which this richness threads.
Not flight, but flowing.

What is there to understand?
The world, this world
happens to us, whether we
make sense of it or not. Blessed

abandonment: strict
surrender.

The Merchant from Enkhuizen

with his sack of kidney beans comes straight
from Dostoevski. He needs to learn the language
for commercial purposes. Not Chekhov's or Pushkin's Russian
but the words for seed catalogues, ledgers, price and volume.
For this, thank God: we can't eat *The Cherry Orchard*.

No Jews allowed in greengrocers' shops, or market stalls.
A fistful of beans for the price of a cow. Unless

you come across the merchant from Enkhuizen,
selling beans to us Yellowstars
for the price of beans, not diamonds.

He hands me a slice of cheese on bread
he has baked himself. Takes dictation,
reads aloud, as if we were just two
human beings together, each of us

made in God's image.

In the Bathroom

Never divide the great longing
into a host of small satisfactions.

Face slathered in cold cream,
feet firm on the coconut matting
(the two small dents
my knees have carved)
I know
I shall never marry.

Cranes and chrysanthemums
on my Japanese kimono,
its belt snug at my waist.

I don't think I have to put up
with one other person for life,
just with myself and with God.

Han

The flesh and only the flesh
...every lust summoned from its depths.

No longer my lover: a friend,
bed-partner, assuager
of appetite.

Let me warm you
with my body, let me pamper all
your small lusts.

For the times I lay naked
on the Persian rug beside the stove,
its flame our only light, and you
the man-at-hand: mere instrument.

For the times I sobbed into your armpit,
as you lay, happy and whole,
stretched out beside little

hypocrite me, pleasured
and desolate, still
wanting him so—

Scarcely younger than my father,
you and he.

My sentence:
to watch fiery and passionate lovers turn,
bit by bit, into old men.

Love

above the sheets, out-
side the skin:

this love I cannot own.
Always reaching.

Through the needle's eye
of an embrace it slips.

Open my hands: it flies.
All I hold is lack.

No means to say or show this love.
The vault of my heart: locked fingers.

Fallow

Rooted in this life
as in this earth, this
difficult soil, blood-watered,
paved with boot leather.

Immaterial anchorage
needful as air: my soul
splits the clay I root in;

floods field, steppe. Yet all
through the rich, the heavy dark
roots' thin, white needlework.

Filaments eclipse themselves:
no conditions,
no desires—

fallow.

Beethovenstraat

Man on a bicycle in Beethovenstraat—
what history book will spare you a footnote?
How your star sings gold on your chest
(saffron, colour of radiance).

History and poetry
have little to say to one another,
and it's true, my enchantment
glosses over so much. My brother,
for instance, his dirty raincoat, his star
frayed, flapping like a sick crow.

You wear yours like a sun in
that sky they can't steal. Our souls
as free as our bodies are barred.

To refuse
to weep, shriek, firework rage;
to believe in God, to believe in man,
to believe in self

without apology or argument.

Bombs and Bach

In another room, *The Goldberg Variations,* while
someone in yet another room
(next door, from the sound of it)
shoots at bombers overhead.

pianissimo-ack-ack

In all the anywheres
of Europe, houses crumpling like accordions,
demented percussion.

I lie back, listening to Bach take on
the bombers.
Needle skips, stutters, yet,
Bach, meaning *stream.*

No miracle of nature: just
one of us, as *Bruder Hitler*
is one of us. How can we fear
what we ourselves have made, or made up?
Something close to us
as the breath ruffling our lungs:

a stream, a scream.
No monsters. No miracles.
Just us.

The Bread Bin

I pursue my appetites to their most secret
and hidden lairs, and try to root them out.

Bernard sneaks an extra sandwich.
I turn on him as if he'd robbed the bank.
Bernard, half-starving, still-growing.

What I'd give for a good slice of bread thick with butter,
sprinkled with chocolate. Especially
bad at night, these cravings
for Bernard's sandwich.

I am not growing,
nor am I starved. And I know
I'll feel the worse for it in the morning.

Heel broken from a grey loaf.
Cucumber shaving, a
smear of tomato.

On imagination's tray
a cup of cocoa:
dreams dark as coffee beans.

Contentment

Longing is always greater than satisfaction...
But there are moments when there is neither
satisfaction nor longing.

Cross-legged, by the stove, I read Rilke.
Han smokes his pipe
over the evening paper.

"Hello, my dear old friend."
"Hello, old girl."

These long, lovely silences
in all this clanging,
as if our hearts had kissed.

Roof over our heads,
food in our bellies,
stove licking our skins.

Lament

And if you have given sorrow the space
its gentle origins demand,
then you may truly say: life
is beautiful, and rich.

I would be earth, but am only sand
the wind scatters.

Let the airplane over my head
drop its bomb, douse my life.
How much easier not to go on.

Cycling with this stone
in my basket, this foundling
swaddled in misery:

unwrap it, put it to your breast,
make sorrow the way you once
made love.

Soul

that discredited word, meaning
all that's disinterested,
dead to the urge to possess.

A soul is forged from fire,
rock crystal, is

tender as an eyelash.
A small closed-in centre
to which I describe the world outside
as I would to a blind man.

A vast, empty plain,
a vast, ripening cornfield
holding something
of God and Love.

Skating Club, South Amsterdam

Along the quay, a breeze
like a warm mist,
a long drink of water.

Lilacs purse their purple horns,
more fruit than flower.
On the rose bushes
buds like baby teeth.

Sun combing my hair,
German soldiers, drilling.

Bicycle Thieves

Yellowstars are now forbidden bicycles
as well as trams.

Bicycle that was all my zest,
my north and south, my east, my west...

Braving all winds, wild horse
only I could tame.

I consign you to rust
and quiet, in a sadness worse
than any *animal post coitum.*

Taking what comes to me.
No picking, no choosing.

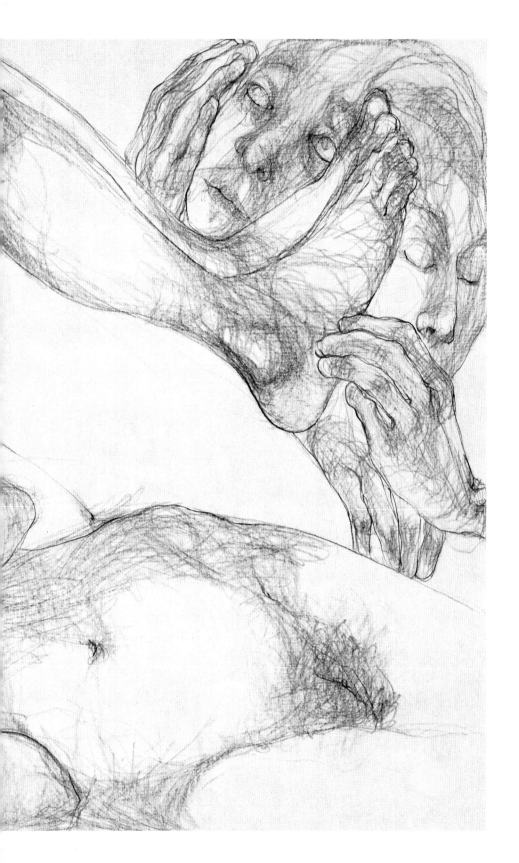

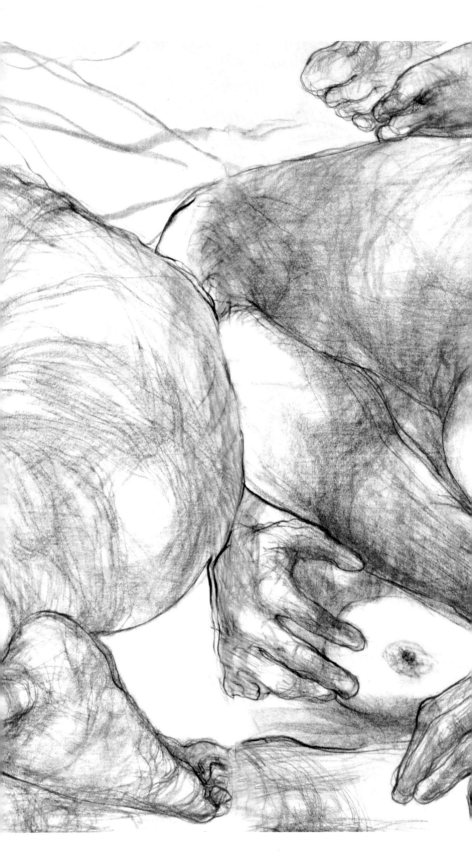

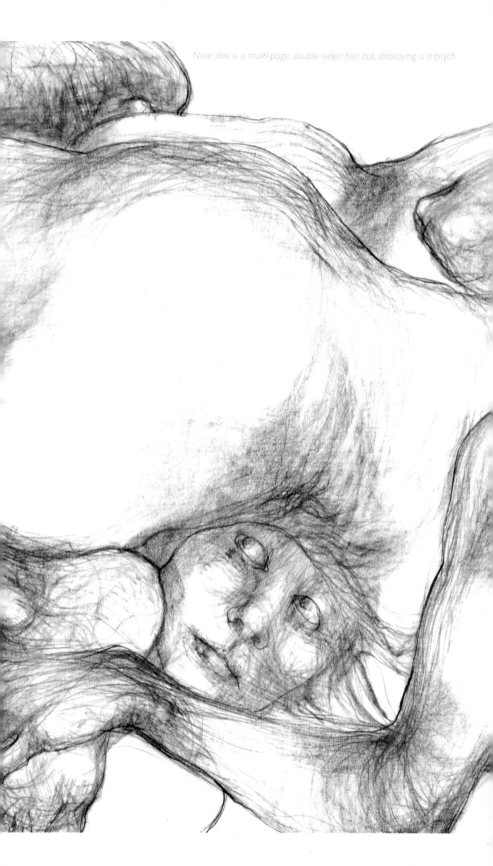

Suffering

Patience and suffering
mean the same thing, or else
patience is what confers
dignity upon suffering.

To bear this great weight
without burdening others.
To grow stronger through the bearing,
carrying my blood in drops of lead.

Strength that will never desert you, though
you would die, in three days, in a labour camp.

It is possible to create...by simply "molding"
one's inner life. And that, too, is a deed.

Wisdom

I who have decided to love mankind
instead of men,

to love life's contradictions,
impossibilities.

I who have grown into a fine old
philosopher, when suddenly

the telephone rings, his voice
prickling the length of my neck.

Or he teases me, calls me
sweet little goose
and my heart careens.

What we love in another
is the life in that person;
that is why we must never
seek to possess him.

sweet little goose

At the Dentist's

A touch of the bordello, these purple,
velvet chairs. Here, *The Book of Hours*
keeps me perfect company.

The dentist's drill a perverse indulgence.
Plugging holes
with silver & mercury bullets.

No lament, no complaint
for the time spent here, or at
the hairdresser's, or clearing up
after breakfast.

To be inside each moment,
however unmomentous: to be alive.

Despair I

No rejoicing in You today.
No great noise. My happiness
drags round in stone shoes
and a coat of bruised metal.

Even the trees outside my window.
Nothing but deadwood, now:
splinters in sky's eye.

Inside me, a lump,
Heavy, stagnant.

Ashes cake my heart. My face
a salted fish. Each bone a sieve
catching every grief.

Desiderata

Inner clarity, inner certainty,
harmony of spirit.

Patience and steadfastness.
Loyalty to myself: the courage
to brave the contempt of others,
their ridicule at how seriously
I take myself.

Insignificance. Humility.
Consistency between actions and ideals.
Solitariness (needing
neither mate nor lover).
Detachment. Freedom.

To make the difficult thing easy
without it becoming an untruth.
To find things out for myself—no
royal road, no knowledge
leading to power.

To accept myself as I am,
my right to be, as I am.
To chronicle the now.
To live to see the future.

Desk vs Double Bed

Since to breathe is to choose;
since crisis is our very air,
I make my choice.

The writing of a small piece of prose,
or a conversation about fundamental
life-and-death matters, a fellow human being
will always give me greater
and more lasting satisfaction than a marriage bed.

Sweet, salty marriage bed:
mere floating dock,
no port or harbour.

My only haven: a wooden plank
snowed with papers. A hyacinth
in a chocolate-sprinkles tin.
Pen, ink, notebook
ruled with lines blue as the eyes
of a northern sea.

Infinite waves, perpetual storms
and a paper boat, words
its only ballast.

Despair II

What is at stake is our impending destruction
and annihilation, we can have no more illusions...

How can I admit this into my heart,
that deep well of God in me?
They are out to destroy us completely.

Not just wear us down, sicken us
by arresting those who risk their lives,
bringing us bread bought
with ever-scarcer coins;

not just break us, like so many
tired bones, but shame us, too.
One section of the Jewsh population...
helping to transport the majority
out of the country.

They mean to tamp, then scatter us:
earth to ash. Nobody's dust.

Eros

to drink from the cup of your mouth

Breathing together, heating
myself through, a long
bright burning.

One breath through the two of us.
Apart, I long for you, my skin
torn in two,

long to lie with you when
my body is dressed
in my soul.

You give me all your heart knows
and I want more, want
your whole body in mine.

Dictating a business letter, a report,
your hands caress my breasts and thighs,
even my eyelashes.

Or wrestling, mouths fused, bodies meshed.
Your *small messenger,* not to be budged, till
I take him in hand—and yet,

and yet.
*I would sooner sleep
with books than with men.*

Ethics

We cannot be lax enough in what we demand
 of others and strict enough in what we demand of ourselves.

Always the fascination with burst metal,
burnt bodies. Creatures of adaptation that we are,
even to our own extinction.

If we cannot cry out, if we tame our fury and disgust,
we must gather round a pit of burning skin,
warming ourselves with all we can get used to.

Cry out your horror, but silence hate:
it will choke you to ashes without
the splendour of burning. To call for the death

of all 80 million Germans
because they have the power
to exterminate us—

save your strength for better things.

Family

I want no husband, no children no responsibility
for anyone but myself—and God knows that requires all my strength.

Mother, *mamushka*, refugee
from Russian pogroms, I have watched you
wolfing down soup in your blue lace dress.

Model of all I fear and refuse
to become: moaning, complaining, dressed to the nines,
whose love gushes out in chicken legs and boiled eggs.

I grew up in your madhouse, I
and my two mad brothers—the medical student,
the concert pianist. Eating your chicken soup,
reading Plato with Father.

He vists me now, while he still may,
small man in a checked scarf and crumpled
hat, bearing one,
just one
egg, and a pat of butter.

Father, the delivery man: *ton agathon*
and *oy nebbich.*
Even in the stench of a labour camp
he'd be happy reading Horace.

Mother, Father—let me keep you
as deep in me as I once lay in you.
Let me forgive you the bond
of having brought me here.

Despair III

There isn't a single kind thought in me,
I'm miserable and I hate everybody.

That fortress I build,
stone by slow stone,
with all the faith and courage I own—

Fifteen minutes' grief
can knock it down,
crush its foundations, drag
me under, yet

somehow I wash up
on another shore,
collecting pebbles,
scouting building stones.

Julius

All the logic and power of storms.
I might as well be walking blindfold
in a strange museum. All the breakage!

I can read Rilke on patience
till the cows learn to milk themselves.
Why can't I live the word
for more than an hour?

I want you for my own: now,
here. No pale
fiancée abroad, no harem hangers-on.
I want to own you, all of you

from balding head to false teeth, from
demon-swollen lower lip
to the flag folded beneath
your trouser buttons. And,

for all I cannot have, I want
others to suffer me.

Flowers

I bring them to my desk
as if to an altar: tulip bulbs,
red & white,
freesias, 3 pine cones
from Blaricum heath.

The opening
of a tea rose: proof enough
of the existence of God. Or
drinking the red-not-red
of sweetpeas, lovers' mad-reckless-red.

Cool, starry narcissi; chaste
green and white of snowdrops.
Cornflowers'
blue noon.

In a brown, earthenware pot,
on a small, white table
a forest of twigs, thick and dark enough
to get lost in.

The joy this pain brings,
this beauty.

That Kosher German Soldier

carrying his string bag of carrots &
cauliflowers, instead of a gun; his face
carved with a mouth instead of a screech-hole.

He pushes a note into Liesl's hand: she
reminds him so much of a rabbi's daughter
he had nursed on her deathbed, whole
days and nights.

I shall have to pray for him, too,
as well as for the rabbi.
A uniform plus a face, a voice
equals a soul, and all souls suffer.

No borders between souls.
No mere passport, prayer.

Quarry

No beautiful
schoolgirl's soul. No leaf or petal,
but granite, carved by currents. A workshop
never shut, without tools or engines,
powered only by something

trying to tear free in me,
to praise Your world,
this time, this place:
these blind and giant blocks.

God

I shall never be able to give thanks for my daily bread
when I know that so many others do not have theirs.
But I hope I shall be thankful even if I have, one day,
to go without that daily bread.

A deep well inside me,
choked with grit and stones. How often
must I take my bare hands
to dig You out?

You are not accountable to us.
If You were, how could You
be You? Yet we remain accountable—
how else can we stay human?

When You withdraw from me
every light in my body drowns.
Dawn blacks out the windows.

Listen: I do not
hold You responsible for all this—*if You*
cannot help me to go on
then I shall have to help You.

Packing for Transit

My hair,
thick and waving,
has been cut sensibly short.

Lipstick, rouge, perfume
all thrown away. Pretty blouses:
anything
sheer or silk. Even
aspirin.

In my rucksack, woollen vests, long
underwear, toothbrush,
sponge, an extra pair
of stout shoes.

Joy and faith.
Rilke, St. Augustine,
an exercise book. And when
I can no longer write,
I'll have this one thing left:

to simply lie down and try
to be a prayer.

En route

My hub,
my home:
my desk.

On it
a tea rose,
a typewriter,
a reel of black cotton
a handkerchief—

Leave it.
Leave it all.
Leave it at this.

TWO

Westerbork

For us...it's no longer a question of living,
but of how one is equipped for one's extinction.

Drenthe Heath

is in and of the world, thus
there are flowers here,
yellow gorse and dark blue lupins
overspent, megalithic tombs.

Between barren heath and empty sky
the reeking, wooden barracks:
a village no Potemkin could disguise:
lice and fleas and all their hosts.

500 x 600 metres of mud, indigenous.
It breaks our shoes, eats at our feet.
Sand blown from blameless Saharas
scours our eyes.

Though many die here, it is the living dead
who beseech us, preparing for Transport:
thousands upon thousands of men, women, children,
infants, invalids, the feeble-minded,
the sick and the aged who pass through our hands.

Steel-on-flint shouting of guards,
typewriters battering names, numbers:
the machine-gun fire of bureaucracy.

Artists and intellectuals, men
with professions, prowl the barbed wire,

gutted of all they had or were,
knifed by their shadows.

Emptiness framed
by earth, by sky,
filled only

by what we keep,
inside.

Credo

Whoever enters my innermost heart
I cannot abandon.

Whomever I love in my innermost heart
I must leave free.

I don't fool myself about the real
state of affairs, and I've even dropped the pretense
that I'm out to help others. I shall merely try

to help God as best I can, and if
I succeed in doing that, then I shall be
of some use to others.

Transport *en famille*

I can bear my burden, but not yours.
Mother, father, brother:
if we must travel together,
how can I watch you suffer?

Too much compassion
can be greed. Strive
for the detachment
the dressing shows to the wound.

The Thinking Heart of the Barracks

No books or pictures, here. No bright
shawls, or market flowers. Only

a small patch of sky,
and space enough to fold my hands.

All round me, women, girls,
snoring, sobbing, dreaming out loud.

And the ones who try to keep sane
by starving themselves of thought or feeling—

Though I am nothing but holes in a scraped-out shoe,
though the debris of a whole city drags my head down,

let me catch them, hold them,
think and feel enough for us all.

Stop me from playing, let me work, at last.
Keep me green and fallow.

Each day's horde of being:
nourished, listened to, known.

The Wild West Cabin

of the hospital canteen,
sawn from logs and stumps. Small windows rattle:
through them we see sandbanks, rough grass,
an empty railway truck.

Beyond the barbed wire, green billows
that could be spruce,
young spruce.

Sometimes we pretend we've found our way
to a mining camp in a Klondike

where nothing grows, and the only gold
glows on shallow-rooted teeth

or chill-blained, expendable fingers.

the pitifully thin, incessant wailing of the babies

To be massed, herded—this, already
is extinction. How, in this press,
can heart think, mind feel?

Easy to write in a sun lounge
or at my desk, in the shade of roses.
Needful to write here, now
where raw winds drill the barracks.

So many broken windows, yet the air still stinks.
We fight it down, as we do the sour
and watery soup.

Fleas, split socks, gouged heels
and faces. Sentient human beings,
picking over peas till their souls are small
as the grit in their eyes.

Children without parents
—the lost of the lost—
but worse, the babies dragged from their cots
in a merciless dark. Screams sharp
enough to thread needles.

Jews dragging off Jews. *Jewish big shots*
harvesting the sick and senile:

nothing is spared us,
even the worst
of our own.

Gulls

For a quarter of an hour
stolen from transport lists, ferocious stamps,
the sick and the sick with terror,
Joop and I watch gulls fly over Drenthe heath.

The laws that move them through these huge,
clouded skies were not made in Nüremberg;
have lasted longer than a thousand years.

Clouds darker than the purple lupins,
the impartial, punishing rain.
Black and silver birds
no more captive or free

than our hearts
pumping their stubborn, muscled wings.

THREE

Poland

*A sort of collective term for all
that is unknown about the future.*

Am Ende

The east to which you were so sure
you would travel, Etty: Russia's steppes, Japan:
that east ends here.

Hard *to roll melodiously from God's hand*, now.
To find life meaningful, beautiful, to call God good.
To be master of your inner resources.

This too is life, this *Tod-fabrik*.
If life is struggle, is suffering,
this place roars with life.

All those made in God's image, from babies
to *Musselmänner*. Could God
be a *Musselmann*, a dead-alive too weak to hold,
defend a dish and spoon?

This suffering, inflicted, not chosen,
by a maniac with a toothbrush moustache
and an undescended testicle.

No hunger, no cold, no filth;
no stench, no pain,
no knowing the pain of others
could make you hate.

Did you keep your promises?
To bear every moment.
even the most unimaginable, as it comes.

To pick You up if ever You should
stumble over me.

How I die will show me who I really am

In God's arms, or in His clutches?
Has He room for you and all those others
whose fate you fought to share?

Did you go into hiding,
at the very last, from Him?

There is room for everything in a single life.
For belief in God and a miserable end.

Coda

We left the camp singing—

A message brief enough for a postcard
thrown from a cattle car,
picked up, posted by some
anonymous Samaritan, or just a citizen

punctilious about litter and letters.

What matters now is this rescue
of a scrap of paper written by a woman,

aged 29, ex-secretary to a chirologist,
ex-teacher of Russian, student of God
and man.

A scrap of paper, letters, and seven notebooks
bear witness beyond
a mass grave. Words preserved
like fruit in glass jars. A quicksand
of questions:

If one only becomes creative,
even in one's saddest and most desperate moments,
then surely nothing else matters?
And a creative moment is surely not paid for
too dearly with suffering?

Conté Drawings and Monoprints

• in order of appearance •

Cover: Untitled, tusche on paper, 1985, 99.5cm x 66cm

A Small Silent Voice, conté on paper, 1984, 99.5cm x 66cm (p.xx)

Vortex, conté on paper, 1984, 99.5cm x 66cm (p.9)

She Stands There as if Spun in a Web of Horror,
conté on paper, 1984, 99.5cm x 66cm (p.10)

They Open Up Before Me, conté on paper, 1984, 70cm x 99cm (p.27)

Ich Kannes Nicht Verstchen, Dass Die Rosen Blumen, or
Know Not Why the Roses Bloom, conté on paper, 1984, 99.5cm x 66cm (pp.28/29)

There's Always Been a Splendid View from Here,
conté on paper, 1984, 66cm x 99.5cm (p.30)

Transport Boulevard, conté on paper, 1984, 99.5cm x 66cm (p.56)

The Wailing of the Babies Grows Louder Still...
It Is Almost Too Much to Bear, a Name Occurs to Me, Herod,
conté on paper, 1984, 99.5cm x 66cm (pp.57/58)

I Have Broken My Body Like Bread and Shared It Out
Among Men, conté on paper/triptych, 1984, 300cm x 66cm
(p.60/over a seven page spread fold out)

Untitled, monoprint on paper (detail), 2006, 81cm x 61cm (p.80)

Untitled, monoprint on paper (detail), 2006, 81cm x 61cm (p.90)

Untitled, monoprint on paper (detail), 2006, 81cm x 61cm (p.97)

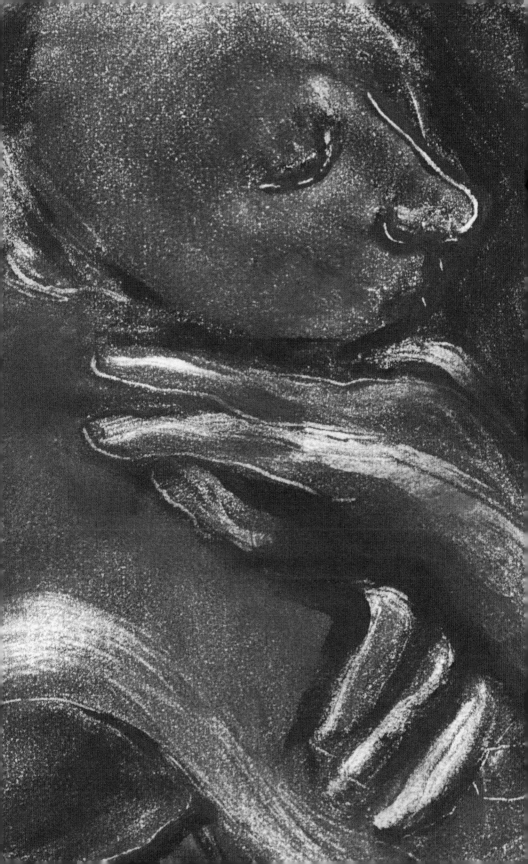

Janice Kulyk Keefer of Toronto is the award-winning author of numerous books of poetry, fiction and non-fiction, including *The Paris-Napoli Express, Transfigurations, Travelling Ladies, Rest Harrow, White of the Lesser Angels, Marrying the Sea, Thieves*, and a memoir, *Honey and Ashes*. She currently teaches literature and theatre in the graduate studies department at the University of Guelph.

Claire Wilks (1933–2017) is a Canadian artist who worked in drawing, brush drawing, lithography, monoprinting, and sculpture in bronze and clay. Her works are in numerous private collections in Canada and abroad, and have been exhibited in the National Gallery of Canada, and in Toronto, Calgary, Stockholm, New York, Jerusalem, Venice, Rome, Zagreb, Mexico City and Monterrey.

Diana Kuprel, PhD, is a Toronto editor and translator. Her translation of Zofia Nalkowska's *Medallions*, short stories and reportages about the Holocaust, was published in 1999 by Northwestern University Press.